Middle C Meets Music Street

written by Katie McKay

Illustrated by Jon Ribera
and Katie McKay

Copyright 2009
All Rights Reserved

To my supportive and talented husband
Wayne for his love, patience and never ending
encouragement.

To my loyal and precious daughters,
MauriAnn Bowles and Heather Lyn Zwygart.

To Mary Fern Petersen
(who inspired me 30 yrs. ago to start this story).

To Hyra Wright for her love and great
insights, and the many students I have
had the privilege of sharing this story with.

I dedicate this book to them all!

Once upon a time there was a little girl named Clarissa. She always wore pigtails in her hair. Her dad got a new job and she had to move to a new city far away. She was sad to leave her friends, but her mother assured her she would make new ones.

In this new city they bought house number 1 on Music Street. This house was right in the middle of the street. Now, this was no ordinary street.

Clarissa noticed that the houses were all divided by black fences and were in groups of two's and three's and only on one side of the street. She also noticed that the houses going up the street from hers looked the same as the houses going down.
"What an unusual place," she thought.

Clarissa really liked her new house. But, she found out that everyone who lived on Music Street played an instrument, except her.

She always wanted to play an instrument, so maybe this was her chance to do just that.

Clarissa didn't know very much about instruments and wondered which one would be best for *her* to learn.

One day she decided to go meet her neighbors <u>UP</u> the street and find out what instruments they play.

She knocked on door number 2, her next door neighbor. Clarissa was very surprised and a bit frightened when a dog opened the door and spoke to her. The dog's voice had a higher pitch than she expected. He was very friendly and welcomed her to the neighborhood.

The dog's name was Dapper Dan and he played the drums. He told her not to be afraid; she would meet many talking animals on this street. He said, "Magical things happen here, especially when we play music together."

Dapper Dan explained that since Clarissa moved into the <u>middle</u> house, everyone would now call her <u>Middle C</u>. Dapper Dan then played her a song on his drums and told her, "Drums are a great rhythm instrument."

Dapper Dan explained there's a difference between beat and rhythm in music. He said, beat is the steady ongoing pulse, while rhythm is a pattern of long and short note values inbetween or on the beat.

He wished Middle C good luck in finding an instrument. Middle C liked talking to the dog and headed <u>UP</u> to the next house. She knocked on door 3....

This time Edna, a talking elephant, answered the door. With a high pitch to her voice, she invited Middle C in. When Middle C asked what instrument she played, she began to cry. Edna said, "I'm too big and clumsy, every instrument I touch I break!"

Middle C gave her a tissue to blow her nose and told her not to cry. She said, "I have to find an instrument and I will help you find one too."

When Edna blew her nose it was so loud it sounded like an English horn. Middle C said, "Edna! Why don't you just play your nose? It sounds great!" Edna was so excited! She was so thankful that Middle C helped her find an instrument she couldn't break. As Middle C left, Edna wished her well in her search for an instrument.

Middle C skipped UP to door 4 excited to see what talking animal lived there. Franky the fox opened the door and when he spoke his voice pitch was even higher.

Franky played a song for Middle C on his flute. He told her that learning an instrument is a great <u>discipline</u>. Middle C didn't know what that word meant. Franky explained that, "If your mom asks you to clean your room and you refuse, then you won't be able to play with your friends. But, if you discipline yourself to clean your room and obey your mom, even when you don't want to, you'll be able to go play. Eventually you'll learn the importance of obeying your mom and *other* rules. We're learning discipline when we control ourselves."

"There are many people in the world who were never taught or never learned to obey rules," said Franky. "They do awful things like steal and hurt others because they can't control themselves. Being disobedient may look fun sometimes, but it <u>never</u> makes anyone happy."

Middle C asked, "What does all that have to do with learning an instrument?" Franky told her, "There will be many times when you won't want to practice. You'll probably complain, think it's too hard and want to play outside with your friends. But, by disciplining yourself to do it anyway, you learn self-control and develop a talent."

He said, "The more you practice, the better you'll get, the more fun you'll have and you'll have something to share." Middle C said, "Hum…I think I want some discipline!"

**Middle C was grateful to Franky for all she learned.
She told him goodbye and went <u>UP</u> to door 5.
Sure enough, when Gladys the giraffe opened
the door and spoke, her voice pitch was
even higher. Middle C thought, "How strange!"**

Gladys plays the guitar. She said that the best thing she liked about learning an instrument was she could be creative and write her own songs.

She taught Middle C that a melody is the tune people sing. If chords (different pitches that blend well together) are added it is called harmony. By adding rhythm the three main elements of music are present; rhythm, melody and harmony. Then add expression and look out, it makes the heart sing!

Middle C left Gladys excited about someday writing her own songs. She hopped UP to door 6 and Andy the alligator answered the door. Middle C realized that as she went higher up the street, the animal's pitch went higher.

Andy plays the accordian and shared his story. He used to be very shy and had no friends until he learned the accordian. He became so good at it he was asked to play for sick kids at the hospital and for the elderly at the nursing home. They loved him and his music. Even though at first he was really scared, he loved doing it, and now he has tons of friends.
He said, "When you have something you can share, serving others brings joy to them and to you. Seeing others so happy makes it all worth while. Music can change our mood. When we feel sad or lonely, hearing or playing great music can cheer us right up!"

As Middle C walked <u>UP</u> to door 7, she was even more determined to learn an instrument. At the door, Bubbles the bear (with a very high pitch) said he was happy she came by.

Bubbles plays the bagpipes and told her it was hard work to learn any instrument. Bagpipes are very hard and many times he wanted to quit, but now he's so grateful he didn't. He said, "Anything worth doing takes consistent effort. Once you start, don't give up. It won't be easy, but it'll be worth it. Music has truly blessed my life."

When Middle C got UP to door 8, she was very shocked to see a human open the door. A girl named Clara invited her in. Clara plays the clarinet and the piano. Middle C told her she loved hearing all the different instruments, but she didn't know which one to choose.

Clara suggested she start with the piano like she had done. She said, "The piano teaches the basics of music and is really the best place to start. Later if you want to learn another instrument, it will be much easier. Plus we need a pianist on Music Street." Clara played such a fun boogie on the piano that Middle C started dancing.

Middle C loved it and said, "Yep, that's what I want to learn, the piano." Clara told her to ask her mom and said, "Moms really like their kids to take piano lessons."

Clara showed Middle C a faster way to learn where the keys are on the piano. She said, "When there's a group of two black fences, there's always a CDE. Say CDE forward and backward, while finding all of them on the entire keyboard.

When you see a group of three black fences, there's always an FGAB. Repeat these 4 letters forward and backward, while finding all of them on the entire keyboard."

Middle C asked Clara, "Who lives in the seven houses down the street from my house and why do their houses look exactly like the ones going up the street only backwards?" Clara explained, "Because we all have an identical twin, but they are the lower pitches and we are the higher pitches. So, when you meet them, their voice pitches will get gradually lower as you go down the street."

Middle C thanked Clara and ran home for dinner. She was so excited about piano lessons and all she had learned that day.

As time went on Middle C learned about a <u>staff</u> tree house where all the characters go to practice together. Each character has a special <u>line</u> or <u>space</u> in the <u>staff</u> tree house that is their spot and no one else's.

Middle C was thrilled when she found out she was right in the middle of the <u>staff</u>. . . imagine that!
She was also the only one on a very short line.

Mr. and Mrs. Clef own the <u>staff</u> tree house.
Mrs. Clef's name is <u>Treble</u>. She takes care of the higher pitches and is always upstairs.
Mr. Clef's name is <u>Bass</u>. He takes care of the lower pitches and is always downstairs.

The Clefs have lived here a very long time. Over the years they have heard many instruments. They assist with the practices and enjoy every pitch they hear. The music street characters love Treble and Bass. They are grateful for their help and especially their yummy *tune* treats!

**And by the Way! Clarissa's mom was thrilled that Clarissa (Middle C) wanted to learn the piano. She rarely had to remind her to practice.
Middle C was on her way to not only learning the piano, but to finding true happiness, and she had her new friends to thank for it!**

The End

MIDDLE C STORY SONG

TREBLE CLEF NOTES

BY
KATIE MCKAY

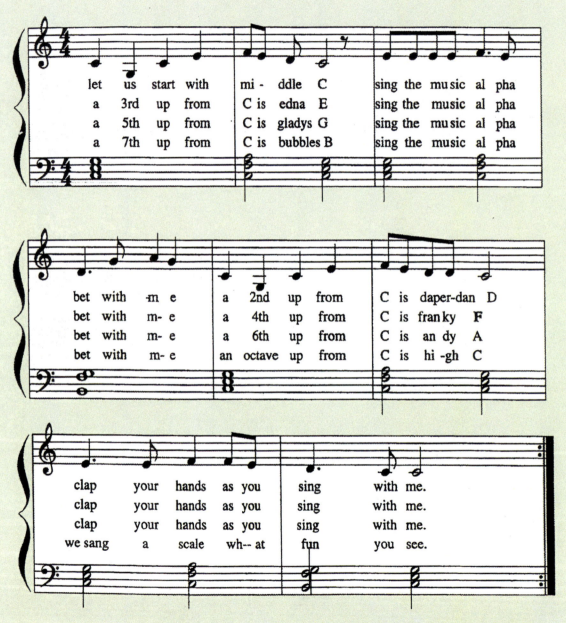

Another idea: in place of the character name and letter, say the space or line and then the letter. (ex. a 2nd up from C is space D or a 3rd up from C is line E) etc.

MIDDLE C STORY SONG

BASS CLEF NOTES

BY KATIE MCKAY

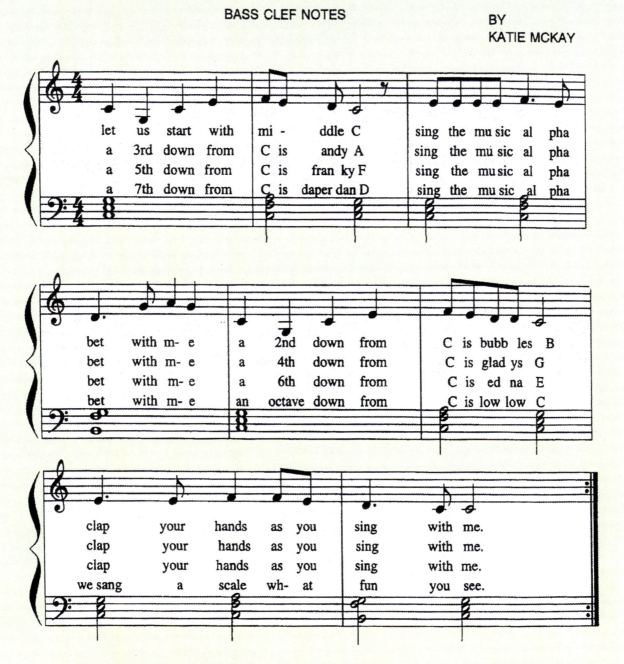

Another idea: in place of the character name and letter, say the space or line and then the letter. (ex. a 2nd down from C is line A or a 3rd down from C is space A) etc.

Katie McKay earned a **Bachelor of Music** from Utah State University in 1994 and a **Master of Music in Education** with a K-12 **Teaching Certification** from the University of Idaho in 2006.

She has taught piano for 33 years and voice for the past 15 years. Katie currently lives in Logan, Utah and teaches general music and Jr. high choir full-time at Thomas Edison Charter School South Campus. She has 15 private students, many of whom are taking voice for credit at USU.

Katie was born in Utah on Dec. 22, 1954 and has lived in Wyoming, Salt Lake City, Kaysville, Ogden, Provo, Logan and Taylor Utah, Joliet Illinois, Eureka Springs Arkansas, Arlington Washington, Moscow Idaho and six months in East London South Africa.

She married her knight in shining armor, Wayne McKay, 35 years ago in 1973. They had two beautiful daughters 15 months apart and are now blessed with ten priceless grandchildren, six girls and four boys. The last of the ten, a grandaughter, was born on her birthday.

Katie is very active in her church, loves to sing, play the piano, teach music, perform with her husband, play softball and ride her bike, especially with her grandkids. Even though she loves being active, another one

of her favorite things to do is read. She appreciates more than ever those writers who have taken time to share their knowledge of music, health, religion and history for her to learn from. Katie also loves to write, and has written two other books, Connected With Strings and Keys to a Musical Heart. These, along with this book can be purchased on Amazon.com or by contacting Katie at kaynotes@gmail.com.

Made in the USA
Las Vegas, NV
26 August 2022